MUTABANI

Francis-Xavier Mukiibi is a poet and performer of Ugandan heritage from North London. He is an alumnus of the Barbican Young Poets programme, the Roundhouse Poetry Collective and the Obsidian Foundation retreat. He was the recipient of an Eric Gregory Award for his debut pamphlet, *Mutabani & [ ]ther Poems*, and won Silver in the Creative Future Writers' Award for 2024. He produced one of 40 short poetry films as part of the Apples and Snakes Future Voices programme. His poems appear in *Under the Radar*, *Propel Magazine*, *Magma* and *Poetry London* among others.

First published in 2025 by Little Betty, an imprint of Bad Betty Press
Cobden Place, Cobden Chambers, Nottingham NG1 2ED

badbettypress.com

PB ISBN: 978-1-913268-80-0
EPUB ISBN: 978-1-913268-81-7

A CIP record of this book is available from the British Library.

Book design by Amy Acre

Supported using public funding by
ARTS COUNCIL ENGLAND
LOTTERY FUNDED

Mutabani & [ ]ther Poems

FRANCIS-XAVIER MUKIIBI

LITTLE BETTY

Selected Luganda Notes

Jjajja – grandparent
Muzeeyi – elderly person

Maama – mother
Taata – (fore)father
Ssenga – paternal aunt
Kojja – maternal uncle

Mutabani – son

Ba- – plural (*bataata, bassenga, bakojja…*)

CONTENTS

A GHAZAL BORN FROM CLAY

Chalk to wall. Date pinned in brick.
Boy takes first breath. Life begins in brick.

Still moonlit outside—still, boy's lashes
fused in clumps, he blinks in brick.

Boy is brought out before Kampala slums, twenty
gather round one cookstove, one kin in brick.

Boy ingests red clay for the first time—
buds against tongue slowly sink in brick.

Like eggshells, clay fragments latch onto chest,
crawl towards neck. As boy is buried within brick,

twenty stay round a stove fire, their pans cast
iron drums, voices in unified tongue sing *Ettofaali*.

Ettofaali. *Ettofaali*. Boy reads [   ] inscribed
on his taata's stone, life already destined for—

MUTABANI

Beneath Bantu sunset
black boy is birthed   burnt   becomes
      red horizon

THE WARMEST PART OF A DUSTY PATHWAY

Maama sends her son through their village,
fingers a nest of rusted 200-shilling coins,
head reciting shopping lists,
heart the warmest part of a dusty pathway.

Bag of milk. Box of eggs. Some chapati. A bread loaf.

He catches the faces of shop owners leaning through
steel shed doors, mudbrick buildings. Toil,
tiredness, grief—years drew battle scars on their faces
clear as the cracks on the pathway he walks on.
They see him. Their cracks widen through smiling lips.
Maama Sara from the shop next door sends him
the best regards of Maama Sanyu from down the road.
How many of these cracked faces had known him
long before he knew himself?

Bag of milk. Box of eggs. Some chapati. A bread loaf.
Maama Sanyu's best regards.

A 200-shilling coin in his hand looks familiar.
He smiles. He is reminded that their village is one body,
a single shop but a vertebra within its backbone,
village hands wrapping around its spinal cord.
Each coin spirals through village hands
as if flicked through a fountain of wishes.

Each child whispers a prayer for prosperity
as the coin passes to the next person. Then the next.
Until it ceases to be a 200-shilling piece—
how can this coin, coated in a mist of wishes,
keep this value placed upon it?

    Bag of milk. Box of eggs. Some chapati. A bread loaf.
    Maama Sanyu's best regards. A prayer.

He walks back through steel sheds, mudbrick buildings,
fingers nesting a wrinkled black bag of goods,
head reciting well wishes from the community,
heart pouring out more prayers for prosperity.

ENVIIRI ZAFFE[1]

Enviiri zaffe climb
   up from scalps, spines lifting
     amongst the snugness
      of Bantu bodies
    rustling in
     & out of slumber.

     Enviiri zaffe cleanse
        themselves in Roman baths
         of morning shea.

        Enviiri zaffe clamp
      onto lusamba benches,
    carry lusamba bowls of
     ebinyebwa,
       muwogo,
        amatooke,
         consume viscid pulp of
        passion fruit
     pulled from summer
        stem.

       Enviiri zaffe clump
      around coal
     fires in the kitchen space,
      chorus

---

[1] Our hair / our coils

Tuweebwa amaanyi
Tuweebwa amaanyi
Olwa enviiri zaffe.

Enviiri zaffe clasp
hands in states of grace, catch
            the coiled winds
of spirits dancing
            amongst the snugness
                        of their bodies.

Of uprooted coils,
            abajaasi,
                        cut
                         before
                        their
                time.

FULL

Father's djembe drum sits beneath a Sahara sun.
Beetles are swallowing djembe drum heartbeats,
turning Father's djembe drum to hardwood carcass
where minced meat splinters are stuck to string.

We watch these beetles play military step marches,
specks of sawdust still nestling against their tongues.
Between djembe drum hearts & hardback casing,
we can't tell you which is the fullest part of a beetle.

We are the boys who sit between playground cages,
our tongues still resting in pitches lined with gravel.

We forge baking gloves from punctured tyres,
pluck the bricks out from church walls,
crush them like breadcrumbs between palms—
this concrete is edible once mould is scraped from its surface.

As we swallow, sinters stick between gaps in our teeth.
By holding Mother's candlestick to our chipped smiles,
whilst oil becomes mouthwash from which we spit Sahara sun,
how long until playground cage tongues are lifted from gravel?

BARBERSHOP PAREIDOLIA

Black boy against black leather watches this barbershop floor.
Thick air saturates with olive scented sheen spray.
Bossman presses *play* on the stereo system, forces

Lingala to drip through loudspeaker buds, pouring
sub-Saharan tongues between pockets of space.
Honeybee clipper chords drag along this barbershop floor,

Bossman points clippers at black boy's afro, which stores
black boy's candlestick bars of ego. As honeybee clippers graze
through his coiled mesh, black boy's eyes track the falling

    strands   landing like coarse ocean waves across sandpit boards.
    They begin to paint the brittle outlines of war-torn faces
    stray afros forge   beard lines bristle   along this barbershop floor

    & then they divide   wilted eyelids & parted lips form
in pockets of space   from these faces   black boy finds faded
       expressions   mourning   mired   bleak   falling

    strands   are coarse ocean teardrops   from gaunt
eyes   that struggle to recognise   their grandchild   whilst shaven
    Bossman sweeps stray black coils onto this barbershop floor
    alongside them   black boy falls

               & falls
          & falls

BRUCE CASTLE: MOTHER TONGUE

After the painting 'Lucius and Montague Hare, Younger Sons of Henry Hare, 2nd Lord Coleraine of Bruce Castle, with an African Servant' by an unknown artist, c.1675-1680[2]

In the kitata of my surroundings,
  place play doh between thumbs,
mould the open shell of horn,
  bruise brown, broken-brass rugged.

At the cape of its root, dig
  forefinger through mould,
lift horn to mouth in damp
  fist, pass breath.

Somewhere, in bump & buzz
  of lips, a phasing through
of inānga strings, engalabi drums,
  boda boda bounce, frantic wings

of nsenene chirping into nightfall.
  Somewhere, maama's maama's
body exists within these rhythms,
  ribcage a bag of loose grains, jangling

bones, broiling from cracked surface.
  Somewhere, maama's maama's
body, baked & creased,
  creases further in my absence. Gust

_____

[2] Google it.

trails through hanging skin—a valiha
          vibrato—expands from her horn-
hollow.   Gust
          enters my grounds, exists

somewhere in chorus, kukaaba, a call for—

Somewhere soon, hear, like natives
          round here, no more from horn

than hollow passing of breath.

AS A MUZEEYI TAKES DAILY HIKES
ON THIS HILLSIDE

Is it here he learns that his sandals
latch onto footprints
laid by bataata?

    Is it here he learns that hillside river flows
    from fathers' salt, their youth instructed
    to halt its mouth from growing
    parched?

        Is it here he learns that footprints
        have fossilised into Stone Tablets, this hillside
        his call to Sinai?

            Is it here he learns that entuuyo—
            sweat—keeps family tree branches
            fertile?

                Is it here he learns that *Okola bulungi*
                dins from bataata tongues, ties itself to him
                through trails?

                    Could it be here he lets himself
                    loose, a boy set free from
                    sling, a fishhook slipped free from
                    bait?

Is it here he learns that impressions sink
further beneath sandals?

Is it here he learns that he is
tree branch—roots writhing into hillside,
footprints a permanent
fix?

SSENGA HOLDS

                                    silence
in the corners where tears once were. To forget
is to remove herself from that which
roots her. How damaging
                                    to shift, detach
                          from spines holding her
    to worms out back in the compound, her father's
                          fathers long since devoured.
His name is
mentioned without cracks,
the tombstone of her uvula already shifted,
     its surrounding earth falling,
                          feeding sweet banana stem,
                              matooke peelings
                          where she sits, browning
                on the concrete. Does she see herself
in the ailing fruit wrapped under leaves,
steaming, mouldered soft? The spines
do not allow her to break
yet, this body
too whole
to crumple.
In the compound,
                          bataata sit on mukeekas–
             flaking at the wailing threads. Ssenga holds
                 plates of matooke; the weight of bone
                      china pulses at her fingertips.

OLUGAMBO

Bakojja are outside by the bonfire. Bible
        pages across its clearing, prayers lance

between gnashing sets of teeth. Breaths
        pause, fearful of what their words might

uncover. Bakojja trade rumours amongst
        themselves, attempt to learn who wrote

which prayer. Jackfruit seeds litter
        compounds. Shields remain unforged.

Once the firing begins, bakojja succumb
        to projectiles, was this always scripture?

AUNTIE(S) PANTOUM

'Pon nightfall, wild jackals rest by graves,
        red skin frayed like whipped sun,
          these holes   far from homes they know.

   Ssenga is still   at the front of church,
   dead skin grey   like whipped sun.

     Dew spots frost around her empty face.

   Bassenga are still at the front of church,
   their bodies   wilted bouquets on her coffin.

Stew pots frost around their empty vase
at supper   *Yali agendereddwamu kufumba…*

        They see wilted bodies & bouquets often—
        will bassenga   see   flowers like they used to
        at supper   *Yali tagendereddwamu kufa…*

'Pon nightfall, while jackals rest by her grave,
        will Ssenga see flowers like she used to—
        this hole   far from home she knew?

* them boy

After Caleb Femi

hatch from black bin bags in
back lanes. them boy

hear cries from abandoned
prams. them boy

hold cigarette campfires upon
metal stairwells.

hold the sirens in their fingers
at birth. them boy

hug the night. night hugs them
boy in grime. them boy

head to the riverbanks. become
fish gilled. gasping. them boy

head back to the towers. find
their tribes from the terraces.

hurl spit. one by one. the same
spot on ground. them boy

hang by bossman's shop. their bikes
like boys of their own. them boy

harvest the skin off chicken bone.
hide their smiles under beef stew pots.

hook tongues towards teeth. keep
them from being twisted. them boy

hate the silence. absence of news
is absence of   them boy

hum requiems from church pews.
just as their aunties do. them boy

hollow
                    them boy

hand back the matchbox. let hands
weave them into wicker men. *

BLOODY WATERS III

Place your father's basin in the kitchen sink,
red tints & white scratches from the years,
the backdrop of your cracked lands beneath its plastic.

Run your butcher's meat through the taps,
the red drips & white fat slips—
like a soul slips between the stained sink of your fingers.

    Hold each of your boys
    like this. Whisper his name
    before it is bathed out of him beneath the rains.

People stop asking what stains you,
when your hands will be washed of this,
assume the butcher's meat of your black body drips its
  bloody water trail where it treks.

    Ask your father if the waters that baptised you carried
      the realest parts of you.

If the flushed-out sin was collected,
mixed with crushed palm ashes into another man,
how would this other half live in this world?

Who's to say he wouldn't have grown like your boys do?
Wouldn't have drained red sin, donned white cap of heaven &—

Rinse out your father's basin.
Watch the waters like red hourglass sands dip.

Is this what destiny is?

MUTISM

Your uncle repeats, "Omwana ggwe, oli bulungi?" awaits your response.
You sit on the bed, alone. Your mother's eyes, urging. Your response:

"..."

Bedroom walls pass tremors from railways. They peel
the baby blue paint. This is how your ends speak to you.

"..."

A VHS tape plays in a corner. Your mother & father run this
for visitors—convince them you had a voice.

"..."

A 4-year-old's cries, familiar, echo from the speakers, fade
into backgrounds alongside wrinkled portraits.

"..."

From a tooth mark in your bed frame, a splinter pokes, asks
whether you also know the feeling of scarcely belonging.

"..."

"…"

"…"

"…"

"…"

Your mother has wondered at times if you exist somewhere between realms of seen & unseen. A ghost child.

Your pillow holds a softcover prayer book, Christ on its back. Your father wonders whether it's a question of faith.

The ghosts may be speaking to you. May be ready to return their hold on your tongue. You try to ask them.

The tape finished a while ago. White noise breaks, prickled, patchy, then stops.

Within the silence, "Omwana ggwe. Ogenda. Kugamba. Ki?" "Child. What. Is. Your. Response?"

HELL IS A DUMP INTO THE PYMMES BROOK

After George Abraham[3]

My black is found   trenched at the base of the Lea
    missing poster bodies   distorted voices beneath which I am
        coarse fuzz of algae coating   the surface quiet

    missing poster bodies   distorted voices beneath   I am
        coarse fuzz of algae coating the surface   quiet
            breathless   succumbing to a mould of purgatory

        coarse fuzz of afro coats the surface   quiet
            breathless   succumbing to a mould of purge
eyes   curdled-milk-yellow   search for God in the fore

            breathless   succumbing to mould   purged
eyes   curdled-milk yellow   search for God   in the fore
sunken bicycles   wheelless   converted into crucifixes

    eyes curdle   milk-yellow   search for a God   in the fore
sunken bicycles   wheelless   convert into crucifixes
        their faint blinking lights the edge of flushed flesh

sunken bicycles   will-less   convert into crucifixes
        their faint blinking lights the edge of flushed flesh
    its birthmark   familiar   is this how out-of-body feels   how I bear

---

[3] This poem is a Markov Sonnet, a form coined by Abraham.

faint blinking lights   the edge of flushed flesh
this birthmark familiar   is this how out-of-body feels how I bear
witness to my body's twists   how it takes shape in wreckage

this birth   familiar   is this how out-of-body feels   how I bear
witness to my body's twists   how it takes shape in wreckage
if I die here in the marshes   the melanated me will hunch up

witness my body's twists   how it takes shape in wreckage
if I die here in the marshes   de-melanated me will hunch up
my limbs   my body becoming traffic-cone-bright

if   I   die   here   in the marshes   de-melanated me will hunch up
my limbs   my body becoming traffic cone   bright
against tarmac noir   as if to say   *turn   lest you wish to become this*

my limbs   my body   become traffic cone   bright
against tarmac noir   as if to say   *turn   lest you wish to become this*
will I be publicly rested   surrounding towers

against tarmac noir   as if to say   *turn   lest you wish to become this*
will I be publicly rested   the surrounding towers
a brick stove from which I burn

BEFORE THE B[A]LL[O]TS, THERE IS BLACKOUT

Out *Hertfordshire, November 2020*

From Waltham Cross   bullet claps are those I mistake for
hailstorm   bonfire   conflicts   a name that exists through
the trickle of history books   to bulletins   midway through
fall   Maama leaves the Cross   her safe haven   finds
herself now missing Kampala   blood stain on roadside   finds
new meaning   split from familiar wounds   Kampala's red clay
becomes redder with every march   Blackout becomes less of a
footnote   the words *#UgandaIsBleeding* slip through my pillows
as I rest here   pray   pray the words aren't reused   ask myself if
this purgatory will shift once she reclaims her home   if I will still
attempt to probe my chest for wounds as if I am a body that opened

Black *Kampala District, November 2020*

From Waltham Cross   **bullet** claps are those I mistake for
hailstorm   bonfire   **conflicts**   a name that exists through
the trickle of history books   to bulletins   midway through
fall   **Maama** leaves the Cross   **her safe haven**   finds
her now missing Kampala   **blood stain on roadside** finds
new meaning   **split** from familiar **wounds**   **Kampala's red** clay
becomes redder with every march   **blackout becomes** less of a
footnote   the words **#UgandaIsBleeding** slip through my pillows
as I **rest here**   **pray**   pray the words aren't reused   ask myself if
this purgatory will shift once **she reclaims her** home   if I **will** still
attempt **to probe** my chest **for wounds** as if I am a body **that opened**

DIG UP BLACK BOY BONES FROM BROWN

Brown as in
cell

he is born into damp overalls   finds
it is no coincidence they are coloured
papaya   as pelican's beak   as dawn

Brown as in
earth

aubergine creeps into his maama's saucepans
its skin wears off into the stew   still
he feels the soiled flesh   as if it drops blood-violet
on his buds   moulds his tongue to marsh   this
is maama's tongue   mourning from her gardens
at the aubergine light of dusk

Brown as in
sewage

on his window   a small mass of bluebottles
punch-drunk by dew   a frosted rose
remains untouched by bugs   is left to frost
further   he hasn't been hugged today
it's been too long to touch

Brown as in
another black boy's skin

pick up
his wrist   cut it clean   count
how many rings it holds

MUTABANI

After Ugochi Nwaogwugwu[4]

Bantu earth
a maama's womb   blood moon calling
                          home the boys that pass

---

[4] This poem is an Ike (*EE-kay*), a pan–African form coined
by Ugochi Nwaogwugwu.

THIS BOWL OF KATOGO IS A STAPLE DISH

Cassava islands swim where lava stew bubbles,
caress these fibres against my tongue,
slope down my neck as I swallow.

Katogo mixes the air with pepper scents,
cumin seeds burst between spaces,
tomato strings through
red clay dust weaving a nest of spices.

> This bowl is my taata's village during kwanjula parties
> where the groom wears a white kanzu woven in silk.

> He presents the mutwalo before the bride's elders.
> Our clansmen cross legs on cracked clay gardens.

> We hold katogo bowls as embuutu drums,
> calloused fingers bounce off
>   drum skins
>   filling
>   gardens
>   with song.

> Katogo's scent is a kiganda woman,
> wears an orange kikoyi,
> dances round the bridge of my nostrils,
> weaves herself through lusamba trees.

Her grazed feet mirror the cracks left against red clay.

Yet still   place footprints to a rhythm of drum skins,
phase between spaces in clouds of dust.

Winter sunlight slips through cracks in these Mayfair blinds.
Extractor fan   & carpet   instead of clay dust   & drum skin.
Colleagues   conversing through tongues unknown to the clansmen.

The bowl of katogo is on the desk before me.
Cassava islands of refuge swim where lava stew bubbles
as source of fire from this winter sun.

I take another spoonful,
stretch these fibres against my tongue like diving boards,
     let stories seam   through streams   of colour.

ACKNOWLEDGEMENTS

Big love to the Bad Betty team and my editor Anja König for accepting this manuscript, spending time with it and showing me the many ways I could hone this work further. Special shout out to Arun Jeetoo, Noah Jacob and Alex Chand for lending their eyes on the manuscript before submission.

I owe so much to the 2024 Eric Gregory Award judges: Raymond Antrobus, Caroline Bird, Wayne Holloway-Smith, Gwyneth Lewis, Eric Ngalle Charles and Joelle Taylor. Submitting this work was a huge leap of faith, and the award was the confidence I needed to bring it out into the world.

Forever grateful to Cecilia Knapp (Roundhouse), Jacob Sam-La Rose (Barbican), Nick Makoha, Victoria Adukwei Bulley, Malika Booker, Dante Micheaux and Raymond (Obsidian Foundation), Owen Craven-Griffiths and the many facilitators that have nurtured, pushed and shaped my writing beyond what I could have imagined.

Big thank you to *Poetry London, zindabad zine, Under the Radar,* flipped eye, Broken Sleep Books, *Magma, Propel Magazine,* Creative Future and BBC Radio 1Xtra for taking on earlier versions of some of these pieces.

Shout out to the collectives and programmes I've been part of, including the Roundhouse Poetry Collective ('22), Barbican Young Poets ('23, '25), Obsidian Foundation Group A ('23) and BBC Words First ('20, '21, '22), for giving me wholesome spaces to birth and refine my poems. Way too many poets to name but know that every one of you is fam to me.

Big up the UniSlam community (especially my Leeds mentees), Process, Everything, Off the Chest, Flow Fridays, Poetic Unity, Grizzly Pear, Apples and Snakes and the various spaces that have allowed me to practise new work and show me what it means to be in community with other poets. You all individually know who you are and all you've done for me.

Special mention to Ellie, Peri, Toyah, Victor, Pèlúmi, Andie and Bhumi among others for continuing to hold and champion me when I've been going through the most. It's meant more to me than you'll ever know.

Love to God, always. Love to my parents and sisters. Love to the clan (paternal and maternal) and all that have passed beyond this life. Love to Ssenga, Jjajja and Uncle—rest well.

www.ingramcontent.com/pod-product-compliance
Ingram Content Group UK Ltd.
Pitfield, Milton Keynes, MK11 3LW, UK
UKHW042150140525
458555UK00002B/113